My First Book of
FRUITS

KIRAN REKHA BANERJI

RED TURTLE
RUPA

AF215355

Published in Red Turtle by
Rupa Publications India Pvt. Ltd 2017
7/16, Ansari Road, Daryaganj
New Delhi 110002

Sales centres:
Allahabad Bengaluru Chennai
Hyderabad Jaipur Kathmandu
Kolkata Mumbai

Text Copyright © Kiran Rekha Banerji 2017
Illustrations Copyright © Rupa Publications India Pvt. Ltd 2017
Design by Roy Creation

The views and opinions expressed in this book are the author's own and the facts are as reported by him/her which have been verified to the extent possible, and the publishers are not in any way liable for the same.

All rights reserved.
No part of this publication may be reproduced, transmitted,
or stored in a retrieval system, in any form or by any means,
electronic, mechanical, photocopying, recording or otherwise,
without the prior permission of the publisher.

ISBN: 978-81-291-4555-0

First impression 2017

10 9 8 7 6 5 4 3 2 1

The moral right of the author has been asserted.

Printed at Shree Maitrey Printech Pvt. Ltd, Noida

This book is sold subject to the condition that it shall not,
by way of trade or otherwise, be lent, resold, hired out,
or otherwise circulated, without the publisher's prior consent,
in any form of binding or cover other than that
in which it is published.

This book belongs to:

....

....

Apple

I am an apple. I am red in colour. Eating an apple a day will always keep you healthy because I have plenty of good vitamins and minerals. Most children love my sweet taste. I am juicy and I hide tiny black seeds inside me. Some of my cousins are of different colours. Do you know their colour?

Apricot

I am an apricot. I am soft and sweet with a big seed hidden inside my pulp. If you break the seed, you will find another seed inside it! I am a rich source of vitamin A which is good for your eyes. I am made into jam. Have you tasted me?

Banana

I am banana, a favourite of monkeys. People love me too. I am the first fruit that babies eat. I am sweet and soft. My family comes in different sizes and colours. I have plenty of minerals that help you to grow big and strong. Do you know that I can be cooked when raw?

Cherry

I am cherry, a small, dark red fruit. I am found in a bunch with four to five of my brothers and sisters. Children enjoy eating me for I am sweet. You should take out my seeds or you will have an aching tummy. I help to keep you healthy. I am added to some of your desserts. Can you name a few?

Guava

I am the greenish yellow, ball-shaped guava with tiny, hard seeds. I am hard at first but grow soft when I am ripe. I can be made into shakes and smoothies. I am a good source of vitamins and minerals to keep you healthy.

Grapes

I am grape, everyone's favourite fruit. I am green, sweet and juicy. My purple and red relatives are sweeter still. We grow in bunches on vines. Most of us don't have a seed inside. I am a good source of vitamins. Do you know where grapes grow?

Kiwi

I am kiwi, the fruit with a soft brown skin. When you remove my skin, I am green and have tiny black seeds. I have a sweet and sour taste. I am a rich source of minerals and vitamins. I can be used in ice creams, shakes and desserts. Do you know that there is a bird called Kiwi? Name the country where it is found.

Litchi

I am litchi, a small, juicy fruit. I hang in a big bunch with many of my cousins. My skin turns deep red when I am ripe. My skin has to be peeled to get to the sweet, white pulp inside. I have a big, brown seed hidden inside the pulp. I am also used in shakes, ice creams and desserts.

Mango

I am the royal mango, the favourite fruit of young and old. I am soft, juicy, yellow and very sweet. I can be eaten both raw and when ripe! I am rich in minerals and vitamins that keep you healthy. I come in many shapes and sizes. I have a big seed or pit, that cannot be eaten. I am also used to make jams, shakes, ice creams and even pickles!

Melon

I am melon, the big, juicy and sweet fruit of summer. I come in different coloured skins, some are yellow and some are pale green. I keep you cool. I provide you with all the necessary minerals and water needed by your body in summer. I am light green or pink inside. I have plenty of seeds which are sometimes dried to make delicious recipes.

Watermelon

I am watermelon, the big round fruit that looks like a football! I have a thick, green outer covering but I am soft and red inside. My sweet juice is refreshing and full of minerals that are good for your health. I have many brown or black seeds in my pulp. These seeds are used in many ways. Find out two such uses.

Mulberry

I am the purple mulberry. Children sometimes call me a caterpillar because of my shape. My red relatives are very sweet but people like me more, both as a fruit and as a juice. I am very useful. My leaves are food for silkworms that give us silk. I am also an excellent source of vitamin C. Do you know why Vitamin C is useful?

Orange

I am an orange with a nice tangy taste. I look like a small ball with an orange skin. I have plenty of vitamin C to keep you safe from cold and cough during winter. Beneath my skin, I have segments that are filled with juice and pulp. Do you know that many desserts, jams and marmalades are made using orange?

Pear

I am pear. I am round at the bottom and slim at the top with a slightly dotted green skin. Some of my relatives have a hard pulp but most of us are soft inside. My seeds look like those of an apple. I am also a rich source of minerals. Do you know that wood of my tree is used to make furniture?

Peach

I am peach. I am yellow and red outside. I have a soft, velvety skin and I grow on the hills. I have a big seed, and there is another one inside it too! You can eat me when I am ripe and sweet to taste. I am used to make tasty drinks and jam too!

Papaya

I am papaya, big and yellow from the outside but deep orange inside. I am sweet to taste. I have plenty of vitamins to keep you healthy. I have a large number of tiny round pepper–like seeds in the centre of my pulp. You can grow more papayas with the help of these seeds. Do you know that many medicines are made from me?

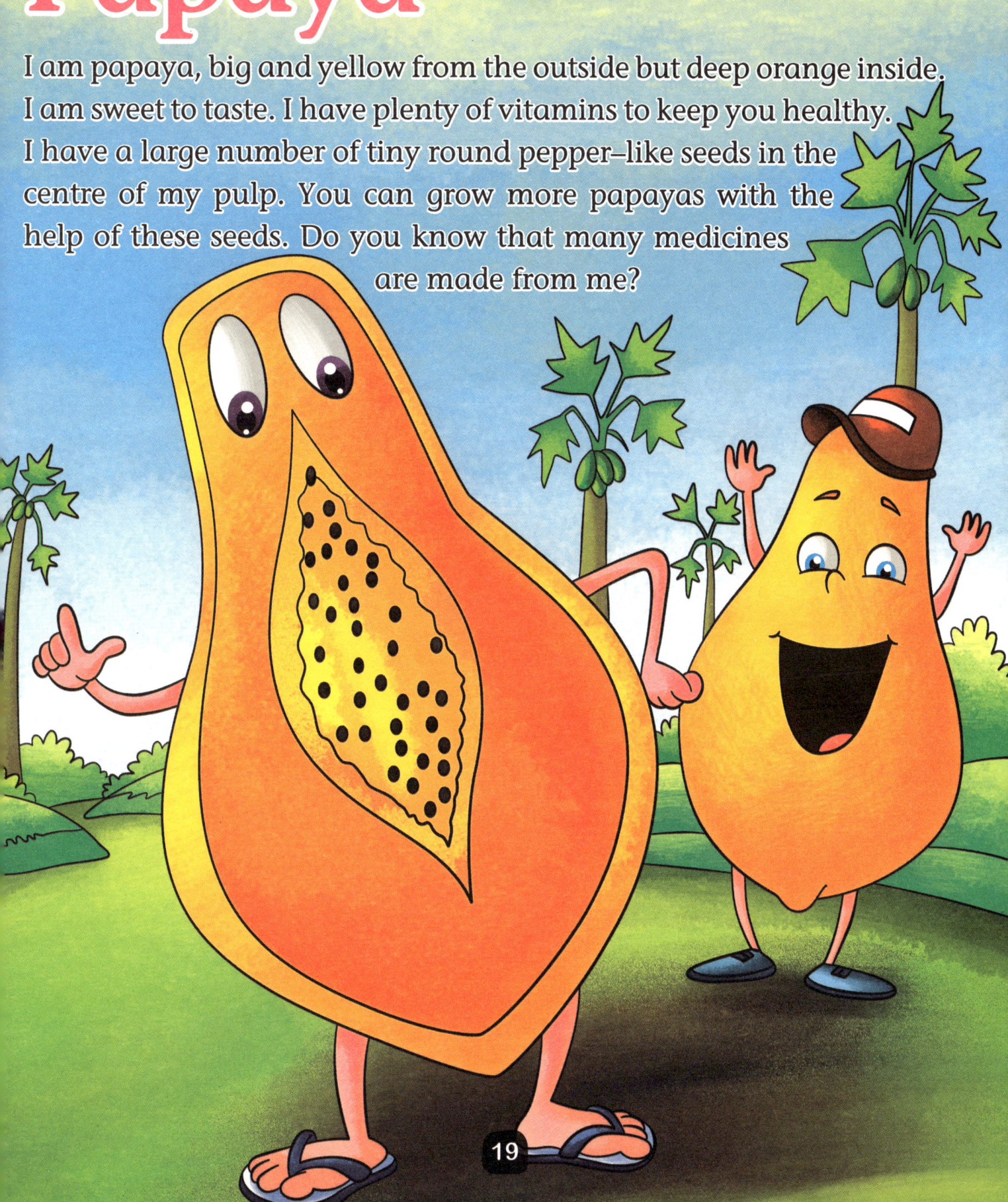

Pineapple

I am pineapple. I am covered in small spines and have a crown of leaves on my head. When fully ripe and peeled, I am yellow in colour. I am sweet and juicy. Many children like to drink my juice or enjoy eating pineapple jam. I am used to make shakes and ice creams. I am also rich in vitamins to keep you healthy.

Plum

I am plum. I am a small, round, deep red fruit with a soft skin. I am juicy with a sweet and sour taste. When my juice is mixed with any other juice, you get a lovely red colour. Do you know that peach and almond are my relatives? I can be used to make jams and even cakes!

Pomegranate

I am pomegranate. I have a thick, red skin and a tiny brown crown on my head. Under my hard skin are a large number of small, sweet and juicy kernels which are extremely good for your health. You can add me to desserts and enjoy me as a fruit as well as a juice. Do you know that doctors prescribe me when people fall ill?

Strawberry

I am a beautiful, deep red fruit called strawberry. When I am ripe and sweet, most children enjoy eating me. I am a rich source of vitamins and minerals. I can also be made into smoothies and ice creams. Do you know that I am one of the most popular flavours used in food?

Identify the fruits.

_____

_____

_____

_____

_____

_____

Match the correct pairs.

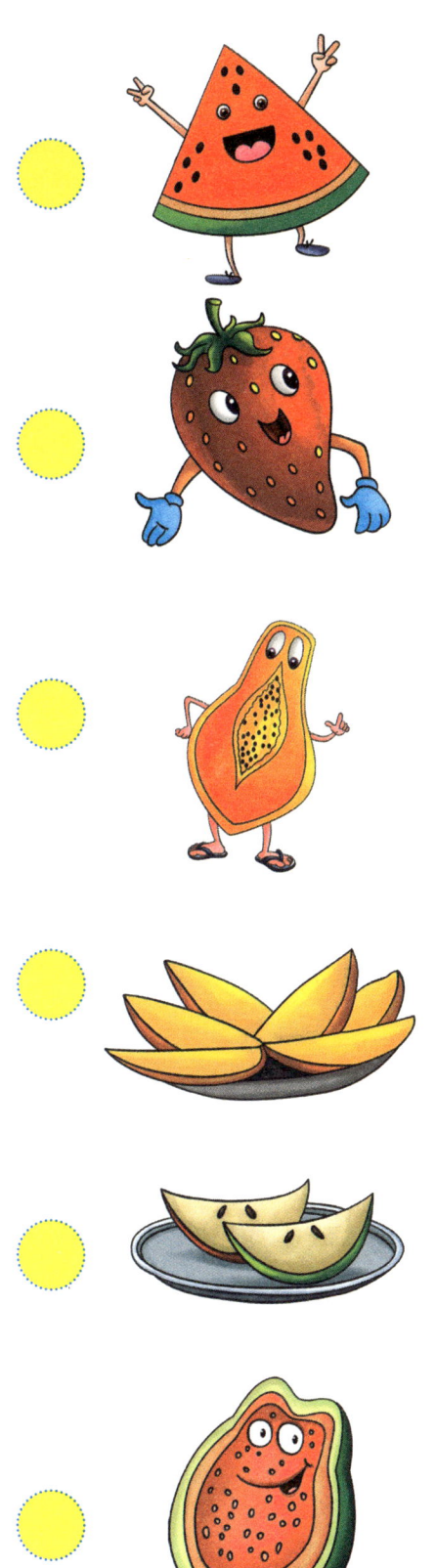

Name the fruits in each section.

Match the fruits with their colour.

Green

Yellow

Orange

Red

Purple

Count the fruits in each row and write the number in the box.

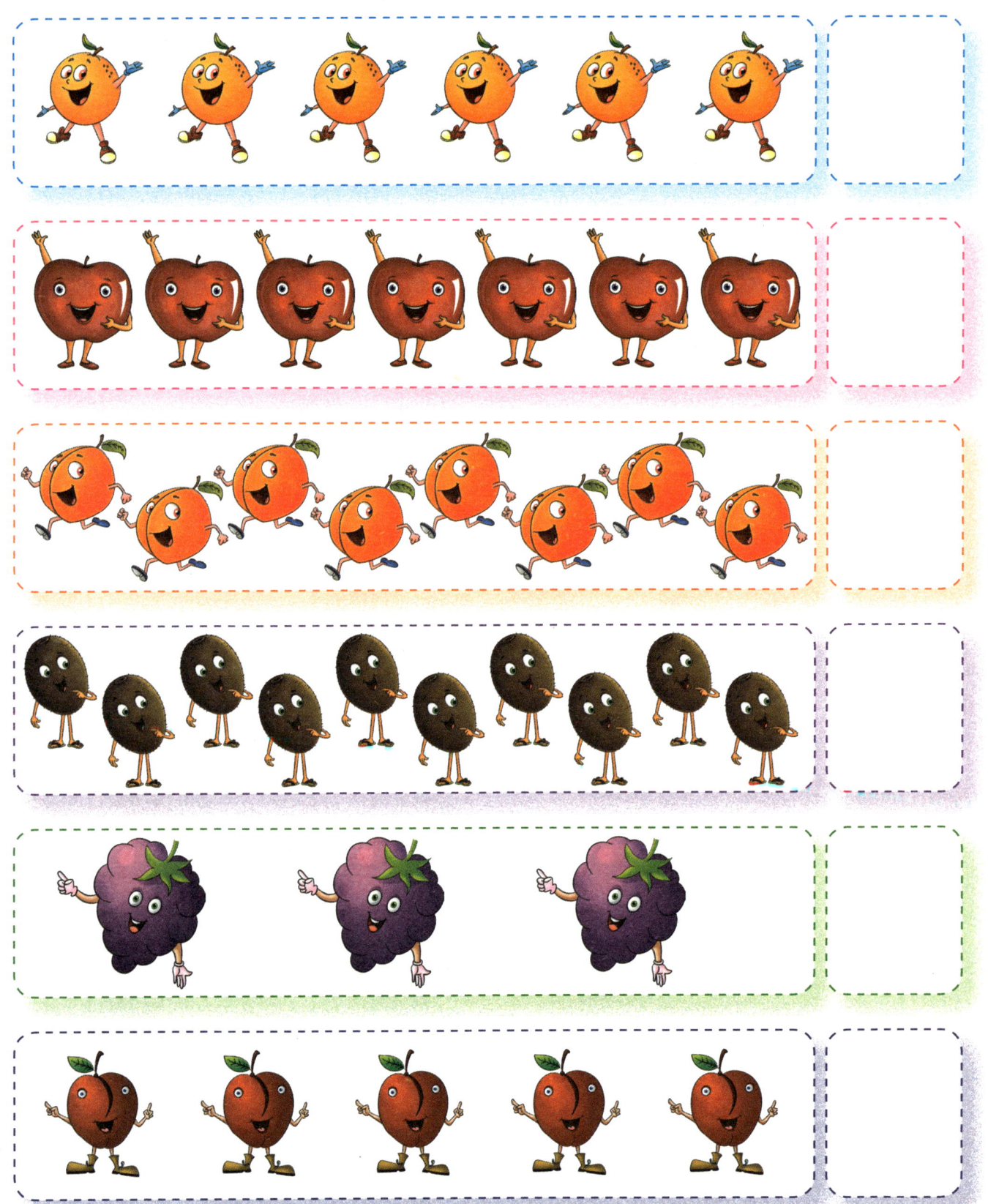

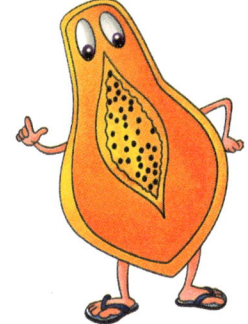

Colour the fruits that are yellow.

1. How many kinds of fruits are in the basket? _____

2. How many fruits are yellow? _____

3. The name of this fruit is also a colour. _____

4. This fruit grows in a bunch. _____

5. This fruit has spines. _____

Draw your favourite fruits.